PAT-A-CAKE

AND OTHER PLAY RHYMES

PAT-A-CAKE

AND OTHER PLAY RHYMES

COMPILED BY

JOANNA COLE AND STEPHANIE CALMENSON

ILLUSTRATED BY **ALAN TIEGREEN**

MORROW JUNIOR BOOKS / NEW YORK

TO THE NEWEST BABIES IN OUR LIVES,

CAMILLA ROTHENBERG
—S.C.

MEGHAN ELIZABETH LAUHOFF
—J.C.

Watercolor and black ink were used for the full-color
artwork. The text type is 14- point Memphis Bold.

Text copyright © 1992 by Joanna Cole and Stephanie Calmenson
Illustrations copyright © 1992 by Alan Tiegreen
William Morrow and Company, Inc.,
1350 Avenue of the Americas,
New York, N.Y. 10019.
Printed in the United States of America.
1 2 3 4 5 6 7 8 9 10
Library of Congress Cataloging-in-Publication Data
Cole, Joanna.
Pat-a-cake and other play rhymes / compiled by Joanna Cole and
Stephanie Calmenson ; illustrated by Alan Tiegreen.
p. cm.
Includes index.
Summary: A collection of nursery rhymes and action rhymes, in such
categories as finger and hand rhymes, tickling rhymes, and knee-and-
foot-riding rhymes.
ISBN 0-688-11038-X.—ISBN 0-688-11039-8 (library bdg.)
1. Nursery rhymes. 2. Children's poetry. [1. Nursery rhymes.
2. Finger play.] I. Calmenson, Stephanie. II. Tiegreen, Alan, ill.
III. Title.
PZ8.3.C673Pat 1992
398.8—dc20 91-32264 CIP AC

CONTENTS

KNEE-AND-FOOT-RIDING RHYMES

DANCING RHYMES

WHERE TO FIND MORE: SOME SOURCES FOR PLAY RHYMES

INDEX OF FIRST LINES

PLAY RHYMES
FOR BABIES AND TODDLERS

Pat-a-cake, pat-a-cake, baker's man,
Bake me a cake as fast as you can.
Roll it and pat it and mark it with *B*,
And put it in the oven for Baby and me!

For many of us, "Pat-a-Cake" was the first game we learned, and so it was the first game we taught our own babies. It is just one of the many tried-and-true games babies love.

In this book, you will find games for every mood and time of day—tickling rhymes, dancing rhymes, toe-and-foot rhymes, finger-and-hand rhymes. It's fun to play "Pitty, Patty, Polt," for example, when you're drying Baby's feet after a bath. "Baby's Nap" is a soothing rhyme before bed. "Two Little Eyes" is a perfect mealtime rhyme. And "Trot Along to Boston" and other knee-riding rhymes are exciting anytime.

When playing with a baby, a little stimulation goes a long way. If your child seems less than eager to play a game, maybe he feels overwhelmed. Try it a different way. For instance, touch the baby softly instead of tickling him, or swing him gently on your ankle instead of bouncing him on your knee.

Even before a child can talk, she is learning language from listening to you. And before a child can walk, she is practicing the movements she will need later on. These simple games, which combine physical play with imaginative words, are perfect for developing babies and toddlers. And, best of all, they're fun!

 # PAT-A-CAKE

Pat-a-cake, pat-a-cake, baker's man,
Bake me a cake as fast as you can.

Roll it

and pat it

and mark it with *B*.

And put it in the oven for Baby and me.

THIS LITTLE COW

This little cow eats grass.

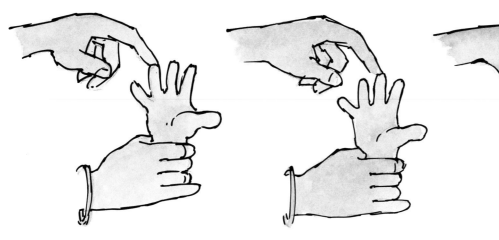

This little cow
eats hay.

This little cow
looks over the hedge.

This little cow
runs away.

And this **BIG** cow does nothing at all
But lie in the fields all day!
Let's chase her
      And chase her
            And chase her!

 # BABY'S NAP

This is Baby ready for a nap.

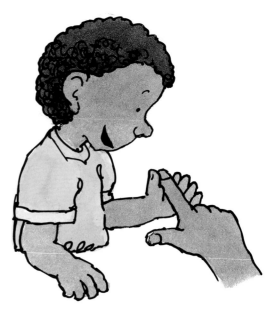

Lay Baby down in a loving lap.

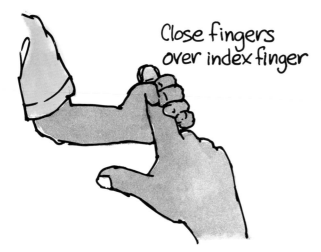

Close fingers over index finger

Cover Baby so he won't peep.

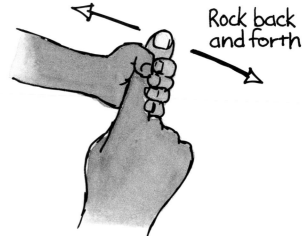

Rock back and forth

Rock Baby till he's fast asleep.

FOXY'S HOLE

Put your finger in Foxy's hole.
Foxy's not at home.

Foxy's at the back door,
Picking on a bone.

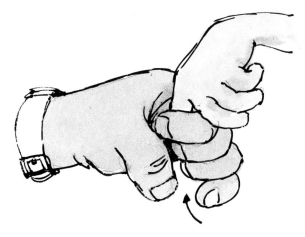

Gently "nip" Baby's finger
with your little finger

HERE IS BABY'S BALL

Here is Baby's ball,
Big and soft and round.

Here is Baby's hammer.
See how it can pound.

Here is Baby's trumpet,
Tootle-tootle-too.

Here is Baby's favorite game.
It's called Peek-a-Boo!

THESE ARE BABY'S FINGERS

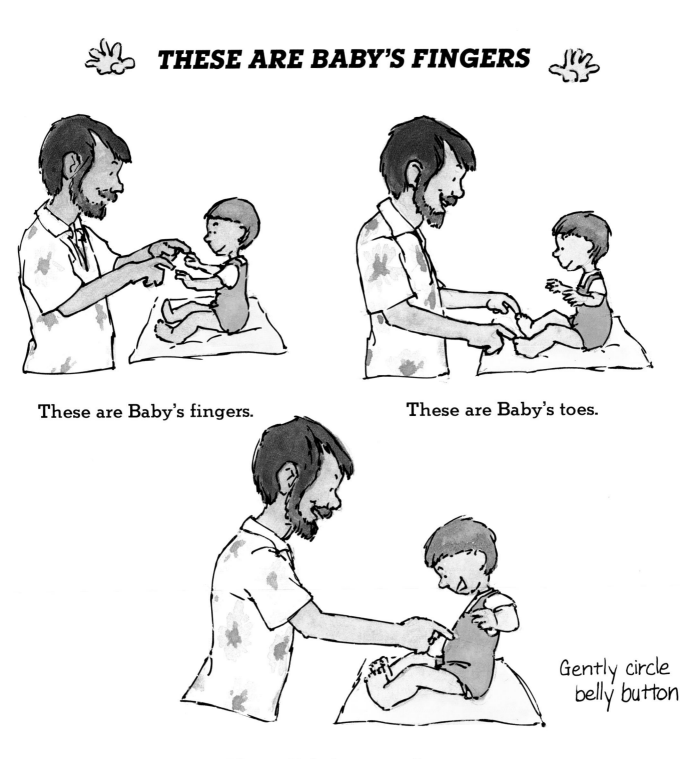

These are Baby's fingers.

These are Baby's toes.

Gently circle
belly button

This is Baby's tummy button.
Round and round it goes.

SEE MY TEN FINGERS

See my ten fingers dance and play.
Ten fingers dance for me today.

See my ten toes dance and play.
Ten toes dance for me today.

THIS LITTLE PIGGY

This little piggy went to market.

This little piggy
stayed home.

This little piggy
had roast beef.

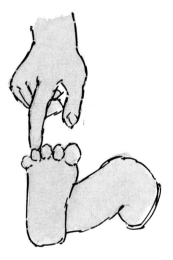

This little piggy
had none.

And this little piggy cried,
Wee, *wee*, *wee*, *wee*,
All the way home.

WEE WIGGY, POKE PIGGY

Wee Wiggy,

Poke Piggy,

Tom Whistle,

John Gristle,

And old BIG GOBBLE,
Gobble, gobble!

LET'S GO TO THE WOOD

"Let's go to the wood," says this pig.
"What will we do?" says that pig.
"Look for my mother," says this pig.
"What will we do?" says that pig.
"Kiss her, kiss her, kiss her!" says this pig.

Touch toes
in same sequence
as in Wee Wiggy
on previous page

1 2 3 4 5

PITTY, PATTY, POLT

Pat soles of Baby's feet
in rhythm

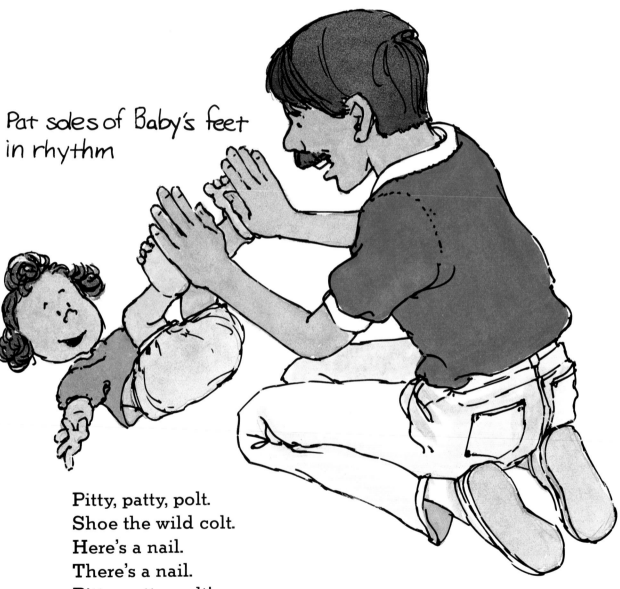

Pitty, patty, polt.
Shoe the wild colt.
Here's a nail.
There's a nail.
Pitty, patty, polt!

SHOE THE LITTLE HORSE

Shoe the little horse.
Shoe the little mare.

But let the little colt
Run bare, bare, bare.

EYE WINKER, TOM TINKER

Gently
touch
eyelid

Eye winker,

Tom tinker,

nose smeller,

mouth eater,

chin chopper,

guzzle whopper!

TWO LITTLE EYES

Two little eyes to look around.

Two little ears to hear each sound.

One little nose to smell what's sweet.

One little mouth that likes to eat.

KNOCK AT THE DOOR

Knock at the door.

Peep in.

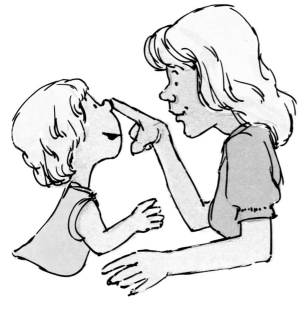

Lift up the latch.

Walk in!

Here sits Farmer Giles.

Here sit his two men.

Here sits the cockadoodle.

Here sits the hen.

Here sit the little chickens.

Here they run in.

Chin chopper,
Chin chopper,
Chin, chin, chin.

CHOP-A-NOSE DAY

My mother and your mother
Went over the way.

Said your mother to my mother,

"It's chop-a-nose day!"

CREEPY MOUSE

Creepy mouse,
Creepy mouse,
All the way up

Creep fingers up
Baby's arm

To Baby's house!

Tickle neck

I'M GOING TO BORE A HOLE

Circle index finger above Baby

I'm going to bore a hole,
And I don't know where.

Make circles smaller

I think I'll bore a hole right...

Poke Baby gently

THERE!

THIS LITTLE TRAIN

This little train ran up the track.
It went *toot, toot*,
And then came back.

Run fingers
up one arm
and back down

Repeat with
other arm

The other train went up the track.
It went *toot, toot*,
And then came back.

ROUND AND ROUND
THE GARDEN

Round and round the garden
Like a teddy bear.
One step, two step,

Tickle you under there!

RIDE A COCK HORSE
TO BANBURY CROSS

Ride a cock horse to Banbury Cross,
To see a fine lady upon a white horse.
Rings on her fingers,
And bells on her toes,
She shall have music
Wherever she goes.

GIDDYAP, HORSIE, TO THE FAIR

Giddyap, horsie, to the fair.
What'll we buy when we get there?
A penny apple and a penny pear.
Giddyap, horsie, to the fair.

THE DOG GOES TO DOVER

Leg over leg,
As the dog goes to Dover.
When he comes to a wall,

Jump! He goes over!

HERE WE GO UP, UP, UP

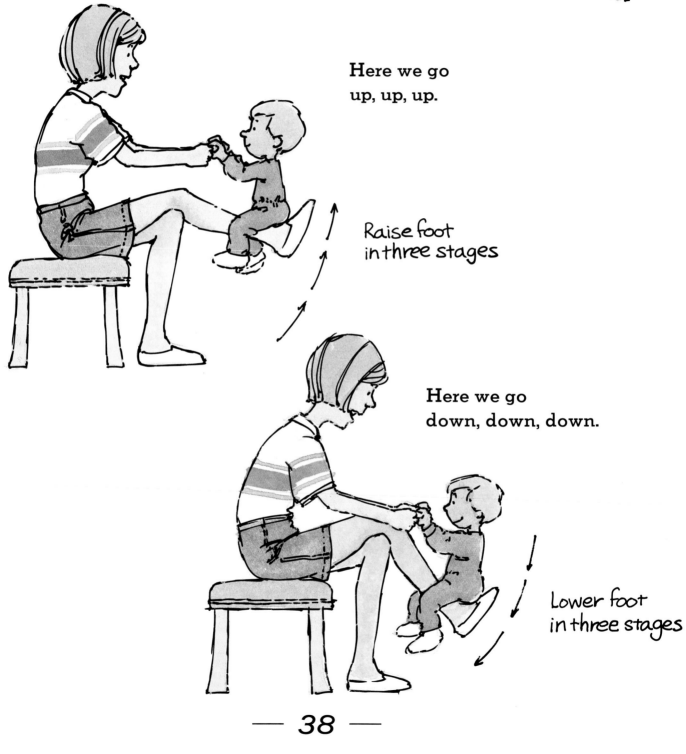

Here we go
up, up, up.

Raise foot
in three stages

Here we go
down, down, down.

Lower foot
in three stages

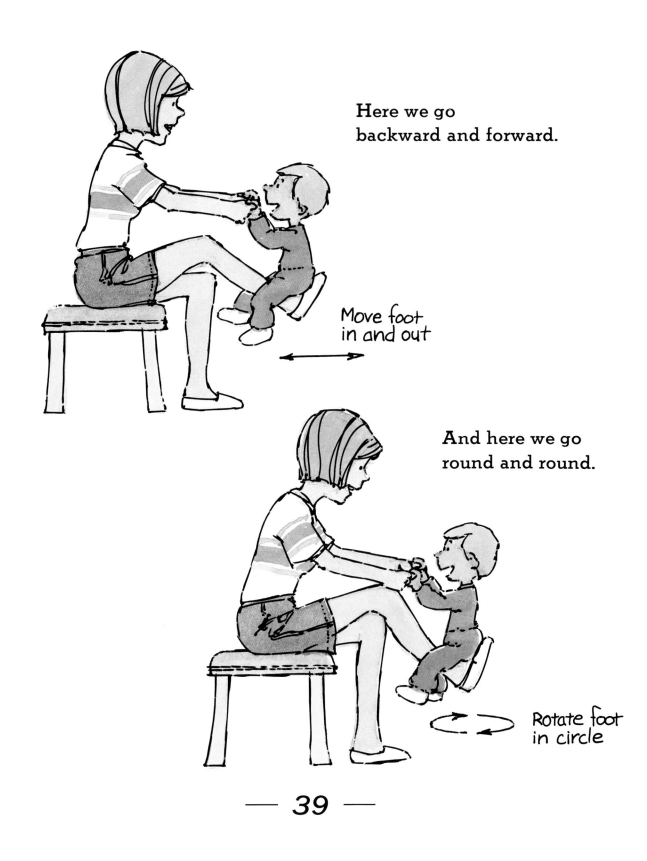

Here we go
backward and forward.

Move foot
in and out

And here we go
round and round.

Rotate foot
in circle

PONY GIRL or PONY BOY

Pony girl, pony girl,
Won't you be my pony girl?
Giddyap, giddyap, giddyap,

WHEE!

My pony girl!

TROT ALONG TO BOSTON

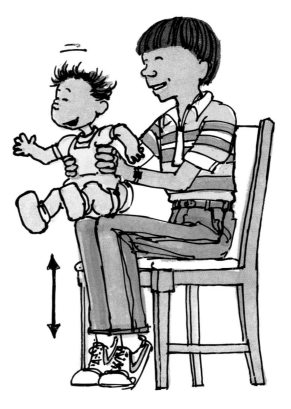

Trot along to Boston.
Trot along to Lynn.
Better watch out,

Or you'll fall in!

FATHER AND MOTHER
AND UNCLE JOHN

Father and Mother and Uncle John
Went to market, one by one.

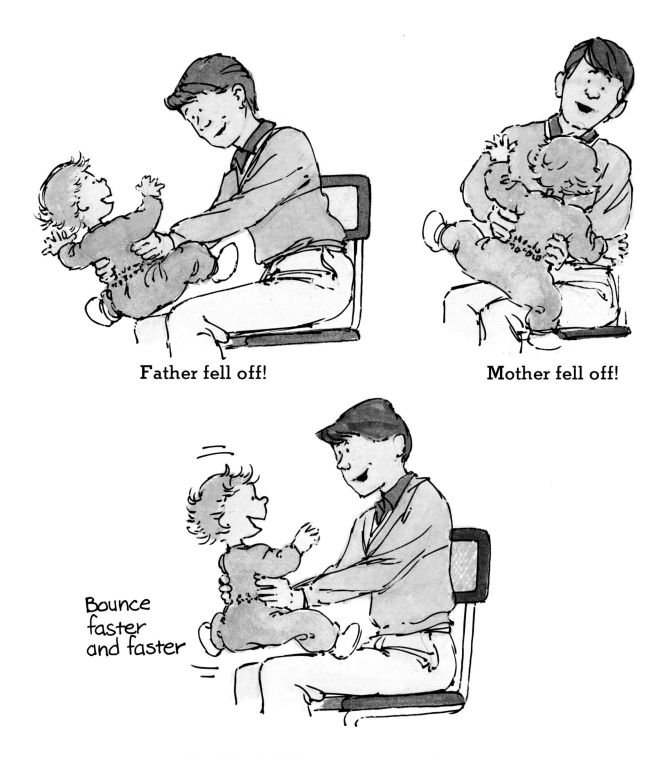

Father fell off!

Mother fell off!

Bounce faster and faster

But Uncle John went on, and on,
And on, and on, and on.

— 43 —

RING AROUND THE ROSIE

Ring around the rosie.
Pocket full of posies.

Ashes, ashes,
We all fall down!

DANCE TO YOUR DADDY

Do a simple dance

Dance to your daddy,
My little Baby.
Dance to your daddy,
My little lamb.
You shall have a fishy
In a little dishy.
You shall have a fishy
When the boat comes in.

WHERE TO FIND MORE:

SOME SOURCES FOR PLAY RHYMES

Cass-Beggs, Barbara, *Your Baby Needs Music* (Vancouver, B.C.: Douglas & McIntyre Ltd., 1978).

Daly, Nicki, *Look at Me* (New York: Viking Penguin, 1986).

de Angeli, Marguerite, *Book of Nursery and Mother Goose Rhymes* (Garden City, N.Y.: Doubleday & Co., Inc., 1953, 1954).

Emerson, Sally, *The Nursery Treasury* (New York: Doubleday & Co., Inc., 1988).

Haas, Carolyn, *Look at Me: Creative Learning Activities for Babies & Toddlers* (Glencoe, Ill.: Chicago Review, 1987).

Hayes, Sarah, *Stamp Your Feet* (New York: Lothrop, Lee & Shepard, 1988).

Kelley, True, *Look, Baby! Listen, Baby! Do, Baby!* (New York: E.P. Dutton, 1987).

Lee, Dennis, *Jelly Belly: Original Nursery Rhymes* (High Holborn, London: Blackie & Son, Ltd., 1983).

Ra, Carol F., *Trot, Trot to Boston* (New York: Lothrop, Lee & Shepard, 1987).

INDEX OF FIRST LINES